WAY

P9-ECS-877

YOUNG PROFILES

Ricky Martin

Paul Joseph
ABDO Publishing Company

visit us at
www.abdopub.com

Published by ABDO Publishing Company 4940 Viking Drive, Edina, Minnesota 55435.
Copyright © 2000 by Abdo Consulting Group, Inc. International copyrights reserved in
all countries. No part of this book may be reproduced in any form without written
permission from the publisher.

Printed in the United States.

Photo credits: AP/Wide World; Shooting Star

Contributing editors: Tamara L. Britton, Kate A. Furlong

Library of Congress Cataloging-in-Publication Data

Joseph, Paul, 1970-
    Ricky Martin / Paul Joseph.
        p. cm. -- (Young profiles)
    Includes index.
    Summary: A biography of the young Latin singer and actor.
    ISBN 1-57765-370-X (hardcover)
    ISBN 1-57765-371-8 (paperback)
    1. Martin, Ricky--Juvenile literature. 2. Singers--Latin America--Biography--
Juvenile literature. [1. Martin, Ricky. 2. Singers. 3. Puerto Ricans--Biography.]
I. Title. II. Series.

ML3930.M328 J67 2000
782.42164'092--dc21
    [B]   99-054361

Contents

Ricky Martin!

Ricky Martin is one of the hottest entertainers in the music business today. He took the world by storm with his hit song, "La Copa de la Vida." Ricky is a talented singer, dancer, and writer. When Ricky is on stage, people can't help but get excited with his **performance**.

Many believe Ricky was an overnight success. But he has spent most of his life in the entertainment business. In 1984, he joined the popular **Latin American** group, Menudo. Before that, he acted in commercials, theater, and television.

Ricky worked hard and had a great desire to succeed in the world of entertainment. When he was a teenager, he was known throughout Latin America. By the time Ricky was in his 20s, he was recognized throughout the world!

Ricky worked hard and never gave up on his dreams. His journey to stardom started on the island of **Puerto Rico**.

*Ricky performs on NBC's Today show
in New York City.*

Profile of Ricky

Full Name: Enrique José Martín Morales

Place of Birth: Hato Rey, Puerto Rico

Date of Birth: December 24, 1971

Height: 6 feet, 1 inch

Weight: 165 pounds

Hair Color: Light Brown

Eye Color: Brown

Family: Mother Nereida Morales; Father Enrique Martín;
Brothers Fernando, Angel, Eric, and Daniel; Sister Vanessa

Pet: Dog

Hobbies: Sleeping, playing the saxophone, reading

Favorite Foods: Cuban and Italian

Favorite Color: Blue

A Beautiful Christmas Gift

Ricky was born on Christmas Eve in 1971. His parents, Enrique Martín and Nereida Morales de Martín, named him Enrique José Martín Morales. But his family called him "Kiki." "That Christmas Eve I received one of the most beautiful Christmas gifts that God has sent me," Ricky's mother said.

Ricky had a very happy childhood, even though his parents divorced when he was two years old. He played sports, went to the beach, hung out with his brothers and friends, and went to school. But one thing set Ricky apart from other children. He loved singing and acting, and he was very good at it.

From the age of six, Ricky knew he wanted to be an entertainer. So, Ricky's dad took him to a **modeling agency**. Because of his talent and good looks, Ricky was cast in his first commercial when he was seven. That commercial was the start for Ricky. Soon he began acting in the theater. But Ricky had his eye on a bigger role.

Ricky was born on the island of Puerto Rico in 1971 and still calls it home.

Getting into the Business

Ricky really wanted to be part of the musical group called Menudo. Menudo was a **Latin American** band made up of several young boys. The big difference between Menudo and other bands was that once a member got to be 15 or 16 years old, he was replaced by someone younger.

Menudo not only made **albums** and did concerts, they also had a hit television show called *La Gente Joven de Menudo*. It was the most popular show in **Puerto Rico**. It was Ricky's dream to be a part of this band.

When the most popular member of the group, Ricky Melendez, had to leave because of his age, Ricky decided to **audition**. The problem was he had to compete against 600 other boys!

After three **auditions**, Ricky was finally asked to join Menudo. Ricky was 12 years old and would soon be leaving home for the first time. His life was about to change forever!

Ricky performing in Menudo.

¡Menudo! ¡Menudo!

"I remember that I had just one dream in life," Ricky said. "And that was to belong in Menudo." Ricky's dream came true on July 10, 1984, when he joined Menudo, one of the most famous bands in the world.

Menudo broke language barriers and music records. They were the first Spanish-speaking pop music group to achieve popularity all over the United States. Their **albums** were recorded in Spanish. Then they recorded their songs in other languages so people all over the world could enjoy their music.

Ricky was excited to be a part of Menudo. But it was a lot of hard work, too. Menudo **toured** the world doing concerts nine months a year. When they weren't touring, they were recording, rehearsing, or appearing on television shows.

Ricky had fame and fortune. He was one of the most popular teenagers in the world. But he had no time for school, sports, reading, television, or just having fun with friends. Ricky traveled so much that he rarely got to see his family. When he was 17, Ricky left Menudo.

Ricky (far right) and the other members of Menudo in 1984.

Ricky Moves to New York

After leaving Menudo, Ricky finished high school. Then, he decided he needed a break from entertaining. Ricky went to New York City to relax. For six months he did nothing but exercise, read, and sleep.

After six months, Ricky was ready to work again. He knew he wanted to continue in the entertainment business. To improve his skills, Ricky took dancing, acting, and singing lessons.

After leaving Menudo, Ricky's first job was in **Mexico**. He was hired for the popular Mexican television show *Mamá Ama el Rock*. He did such a great job on the show that he was given the starring role in *Alcanzar una Estrella II*. Ricky played Pablo, the lead singer in a band. The show was so popular that it was made into a movie. Ricky received an award for his great performance.

The band in the television show was such a hit that it became a real band called Muñecos de Papel. They began to do concerts in **Mexico**. Ricky was the lead singer of this band. He was once again famous throughout **Latin America**.

Ricky was so popular that Sony Records signed him as a solo recording artist. Ricky was on his way to becoming world famous for the second time!

Ricky signs autographs for waiting fans.

Ricky Goes Solo

Ricky's first **album** for Sony Records was titled, *Ricky Martin*. It was released in 1991 and sold more than 500,000 copies around the world. Ricky's album was one of the highest-selling **Latin American debuts** in history.

Ricky played 120 sold-out concerts throughout Latin America. Fans went crazy for Ricky! He won an award as Best New Latin Artist that year. Ricky was very happy to have achieved success as a solo artist.

Ricky's second album was called, *Me Amarás*. This album was even better than the last. Once again, Ricky was a hit. *Me Amarás* sold very well around the world. Ricky was awarded *Billboard's* Best Latin Artist.

After doing concerts for *Me Amarás*, Ricky knew there was other work he wanted to do. Ricky wanted to continue acting.

General Hospital

Ricky was already a popular actor in **Mexico**. But in the United States, he was not well known. In 1994, Ricky got his break in the United States. He was cast in the American **soap opera**, *General Hospital*. Ricky played the character Miguel Morez.

Ricky was very popular as Miguel. He showed terrific acting ability. Unlike Ricky's sunny personality, the character of Miguel was very dark and **moody**. Ricky loved being on *General Hospital* and credits it for making him an American star.

In 1996, Ricky left *General Hospital* to work on **Broadway**. Broadway is an area in New York City that has world famous theaters. It was always Ricky's dream to be on Broadway.

Opposite page: Ricky during his General Hospital *days.*

Ricky on Broadway

Ricky faced the greatest challenge of his career in 1996 when he starred in the play *Les Misérables*. Ricky had an important role in this famous **Broadway** play. *Les Misérables* had been on Broadway for many years. The **producers** were looking for someone to keep it fresh and exciting. That person was Ricky!

Ricky signed on to do *Les Misérables* for three months. At the same time, Ricky released his third **album**, *A Medio Vivir*. It was a very hectic time for Ricky. He had only 11 days to learn all of his lines for the play! He also had to fly to **Spain** for five days to do concerts for his new album.

When Ricky got back from **Spain**, he had three days left before his first **Broadway performance.** He rehearsed from eight in the morning until midnight. He was nervous. But when the curtain went up on opening night, Ricky was ready.

There was a lot of singing and dancing involved in the play, and Ricky did a great job. He received great reviews.

"La Copa de la Vida"

After working on **Broadway,** Ricky turned his attention back to his third solo **album**, *A Medio Vivir*. It was a huge hit. Unlike his first two albums, *A Medio Vivir* was a hit not only in **Latin America**, but also around the world. *A Medio Vivir* went triple platinum! That means it sold over three million copies!

Ricky stayed busy by doing concerts all over the world. Most of the concerts were sold out. Then Ricky put out his next album, *Vuelve*. It was a huge success. It has sold nearly three times as many albums as Ricky's first three albums combined!

Vuelve contained the hit song "La Copa de la Vida." Ricky performed his hit song for a television audience of more than two billion people at the World Cup Soccer Final in Paris!

"La Copa de la Vida" was played on nearly every radio station around the world. It was a number one song in the United States, England, France, and Germany. It was number one in every **Latin American** country. And in Australia, it was number one for six weeks and on the charts for nearly a year!

Ricky performed his song all over the world. He went on to win many awards including a Grammy for Best Latin Pop **Performance**.

Ricky kisses his Grammy for best Latin pop performance for Vuelve *at the 41st Annual Grammy Awards.*

"Livin' la Vida Loca"

All of Ricky's **albums** up to this point had been recorded in Spanish. Ricky wanted to make an English album. In 1999, he released his first English album and called it *Ricky Martin*. Even though his first album already had that title, the record company thought that it would be best to use his name.

The first song released from the album was "Livin' la Vida Loca." It was a hit all over the world. It was number one on the *Billboard* charts two weeks before it was even released! And the video for "Livin' la Vida Loca" won the MTV Awards for Best Dance Video and Best Pop Video.

Ricky now was one
of the biggest
entertainers in the
world. His concerts
were sell outs, he
played on every major
award show, his videos
were the most
requested, and his
music topped the
charts.

Ricky takes home two awards at the 1999
Billboard *Latin Music Awards.*

A Bright Future

Ricky has been a star since he shot his first commercial. He was known around the world before he was even a teenager with the band Menudo. Ricky did movies, television, and even **Broadway!** Now, his solo career is like no other.

Ricky has done it all. He is a great musician, an awesome dancer, and an unbelievable actor. Plus, he can do everything in two languages!

There is no telling where Ricky will go next. The only thing for sure is that with his talent and determination Ricky will be able to do anything he puts his mind to.

Ricky receives the award for World's best-selling Latin artist of the Year at the World Music Awards in 1999.

How to Contact Ricky

Ricky's official Web site is:

www.rickymartin.com

You can email Ricky at:

rickym@coqui.net

You can join Ricky's fan club by writing:

Ricky Martin International
Fan Club
P.O. Box 13345
Santurce Station
San Juan, Puerto Rico

Ricky performs at a concert in Los Angeles.

Glossary

Album: recorded songs put on a tape or disk to be sold and listened to.

Audition: a short performance to show ability in order to get a part in a movie, a play, or a band.

Broadway: a street in New York City that has many theaters. It is world famous for its excellent plays.

Debut: the first appearance.

Latin America: the countries in Central and Southern America. It also includes the West Indies and Mexico.

Mexico: a Spanish-speaking country that borders the United States to the south.

Modeling Agency: a type of business that hires out people to be in commercials, catalogs, or other types of advertisements.

Moody: a person that is gloomy and angry.

Perform: to present entertainment to an audience.

Producers: people that are in charge of a play, television show, movie, or album.

Puerto Rico: an island in the Caribbean, southeast of Florida, that is associated with the United States but is not a state. Its official name is the Commonwealth of Puerto Rico.

Soap Opera: a daytime television show that is on Monday through Friday with a continuing plot.

Spain: a Spanish-speaking country in Europe that borders France and Portugal.

Tour: what entertainers do when they go around the world giving concerts, usually to promote an album.

Pass It On

Tell readers around the country information you've learned about your favorite superstars. Share your little-known facts and interesting stories.
We want to hear from you!
To get posted on the ABDO Publishing Company Web site email us at: Adventure@abdopub.com
Download a free screen saver at www.abdopub.com

Index